PAINT BY STICKER

KIDS

CHRISTMAS

workman

• NEW YORK •

The following images were used to create the low-poly interpretations in this book:

Page 5: Snowflakes
© DVMSimages/dreamstime.com

Page 13: Christmas tree
© Valentina Razumova/dreamstime.com

Page 15: Reindeer
© Vladimir Melnikov/dreamstime.com

Page 19: Nutcracker
© Tracy Decourcy/dreamstime.com

Page 23: Snowman
© Dinorah Alejandra Arizpe Valdés/dreamstime.com

ISBN 978-1-5235-0675-0

Art and design by Claire Torres and Ying Cheng, created with assistance from Phil Conigliaro

Workman books are available at special discounts when purchased in bulk for premiums and sales promotions as well as for fund-raising or educational use. Special editions or book excerpts can also be created to specification. For details, contact the Special Sales Director at the address below, or send an email to specialmarkets@workman.com.

Workman Publishing Co., Inc.
225 Varick Street
New York, NY 10014-4381

workman.com

WORKMAN and PAINT BY STICKER are registered trademarks of Workman Publishing Co., Inc.

Printed in China
First printing August 2019
10 9 8 7 6 5 4 3 2

HOW TO PAINT BY STICKER

1. PICK YOUR IMAGE. Do you want to sticker the jolly Santa or the sparkling snowflakes? It's up to you! Just find the page you want to paint with stickers.

2. FIND YOUR STICKERS. The sticker sheets are in the back of the book. In the top corner of each sheet is an image of a painting page. Find the sticker sheet that goes with the page you want to paint. Both the sticker sheets and the painting pages can be torn out of the book so you don't have to flip back and forth between them.

3. MATCH THE NUMBERS. Each sticker has a number next to it, and each painting page has numbers on it. Match the sticker number with the number on the painting page. Be careful! The stickers aren't removable.

4. WATCH YOUR PAINTING COME TO LIFE! After you've finished your masterpiece, you can frame it, use it as decoration, or give it as a gift.

ARE YOU READY? LET'S START STICKERING!

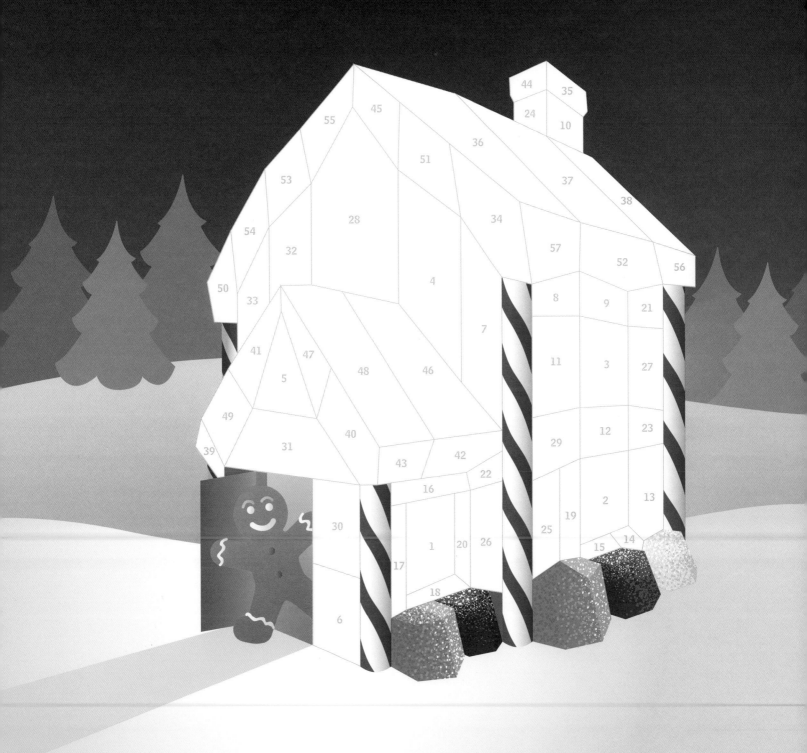

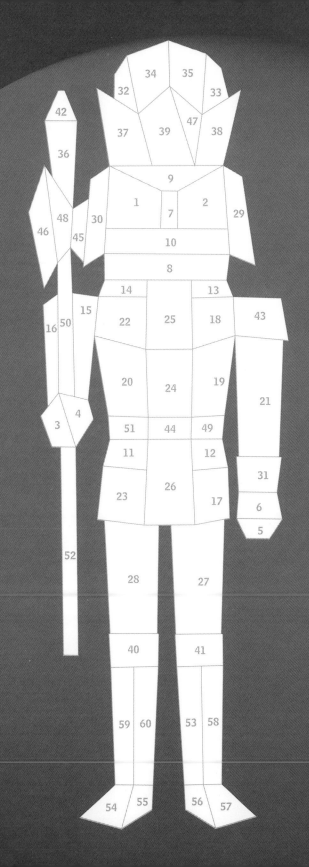

2
4
6
10
11
7
24
26
23
22
27
37
49
51
42
34
35
21
25
18
20
32
40
41
28
36
15
1
13
30
16
5
29
8
14
17
48
19
3
39
59
9
60
12
38
45
33
47
31
55
57
50
44
58
56
46
43
54
53
52

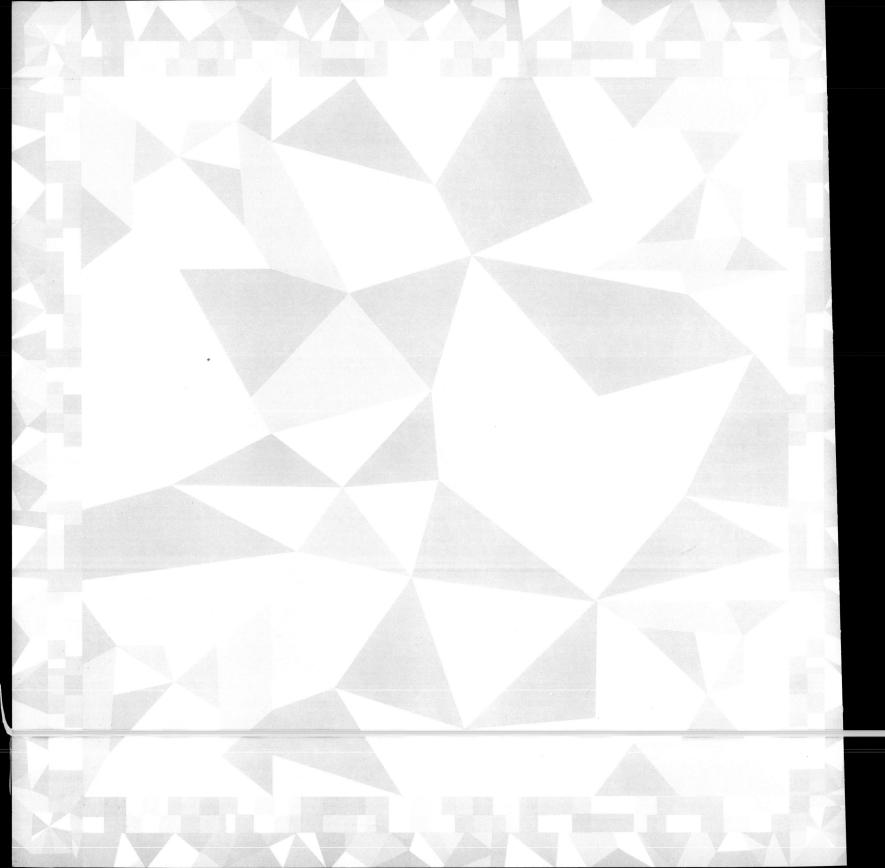

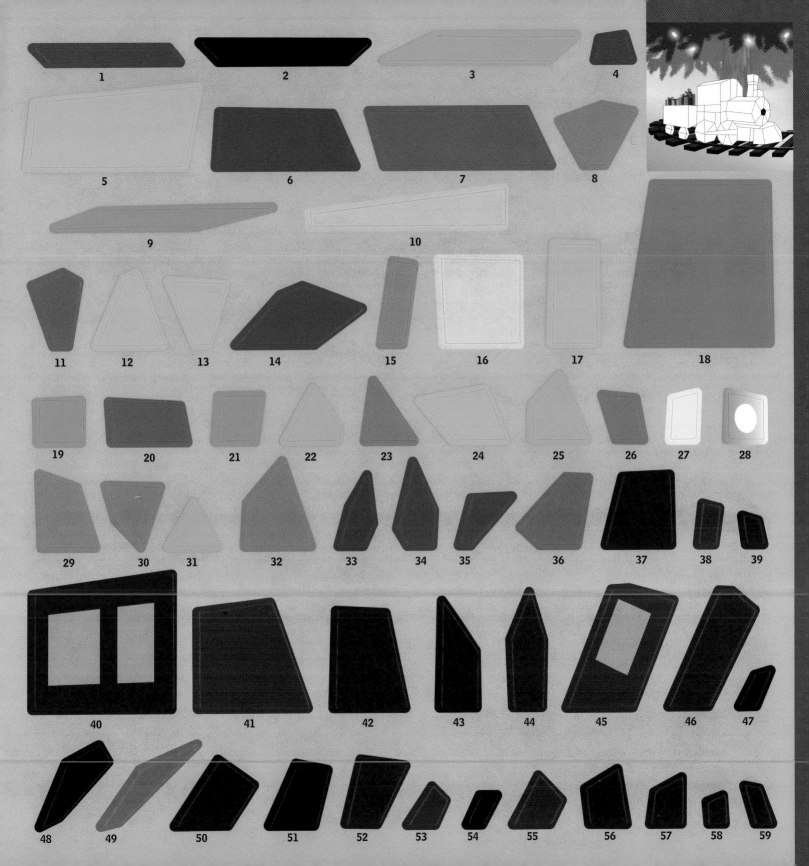

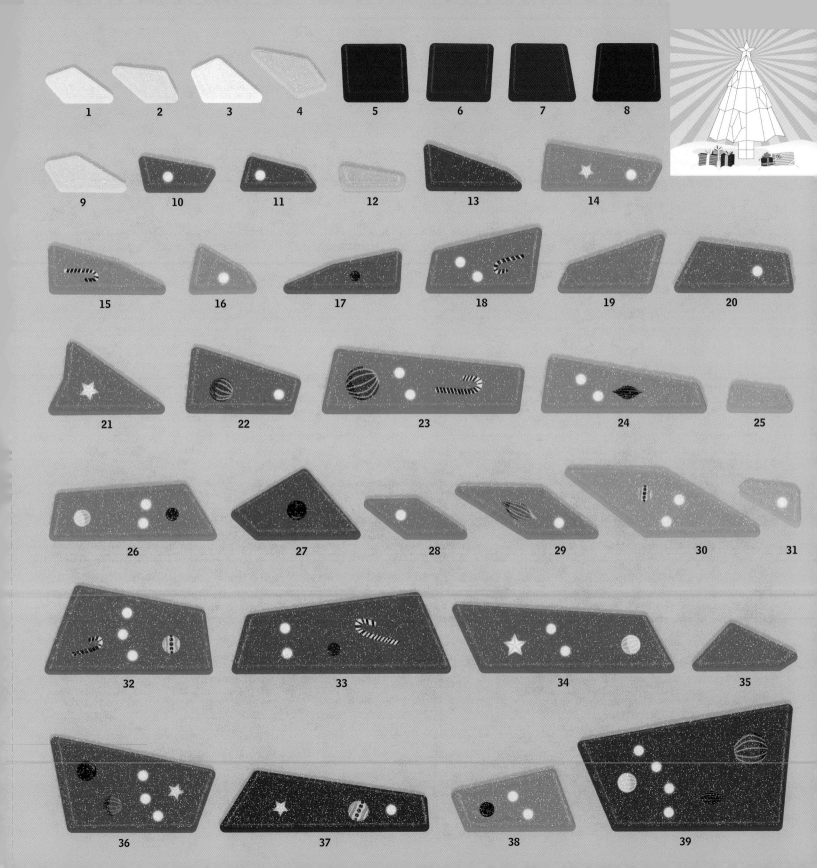

1

2

3

4

5

6

7

8

9

10

11

12

13

14

15

16

17

18

19

20

21

22

23

24

25

26

27

28

29

30

31

32

33

34

35

36

37

38

39

40

41

42

43

44

45

46

47

48

49

50

51

52

53

54

55

56

57

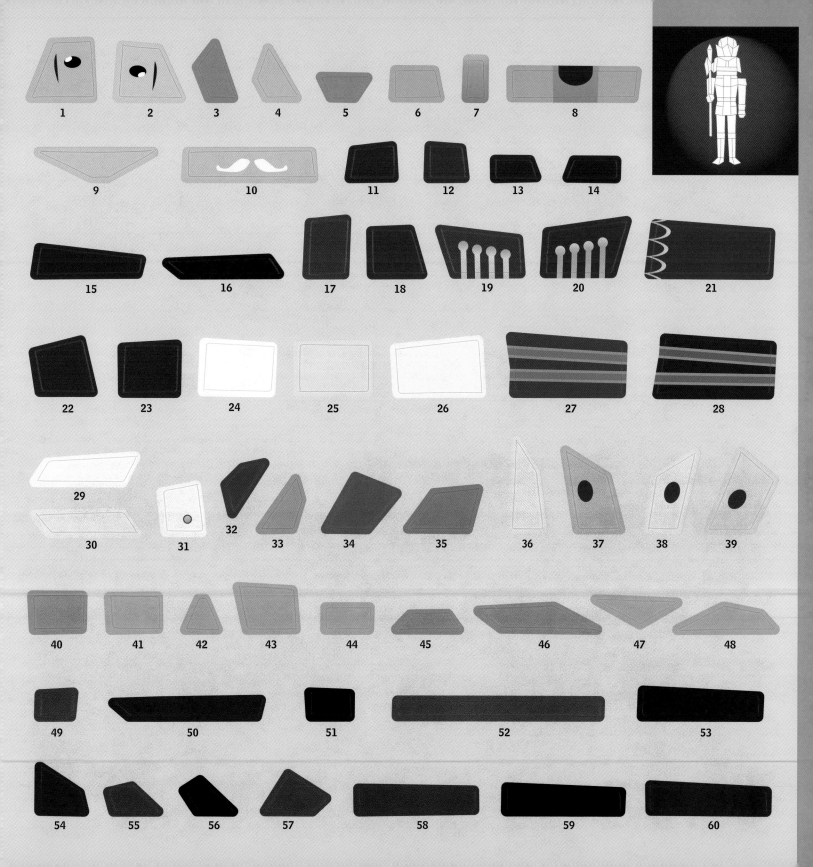

1   2   3   4   5   6   7   8

9   10   11   12   13   14

15   16   17   18   19   20   21

22   23   24   25   26   27   28

29
30   31   32   33   34   35   36   37   38   39

40   41   42   43   44   45   46   47   48

49   50   51   52   53

54   55   56   57   58   59   60

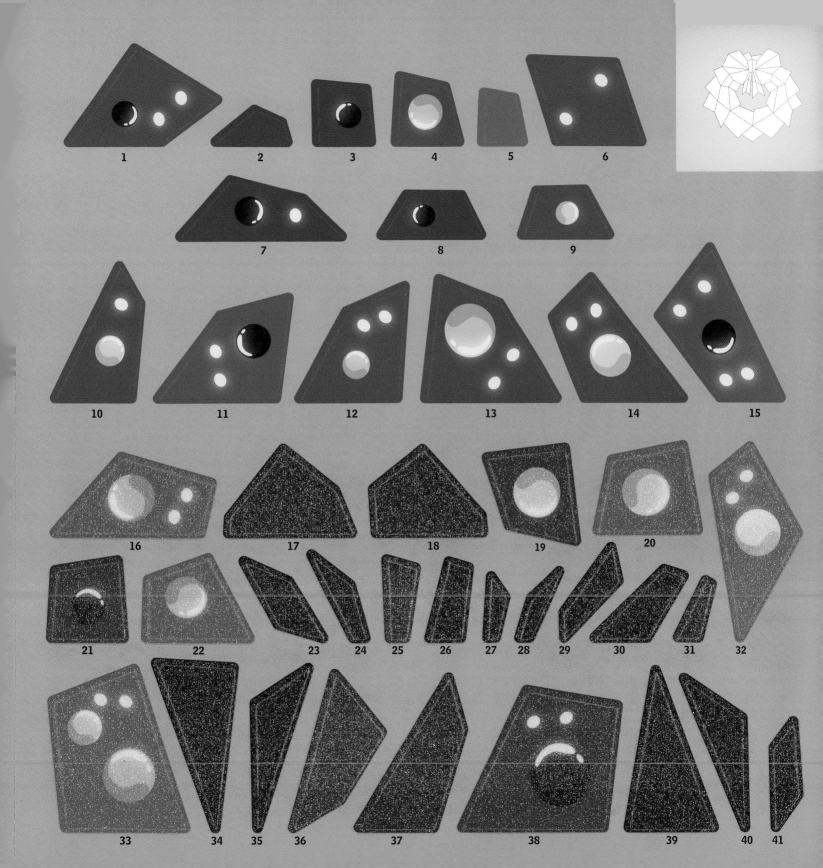

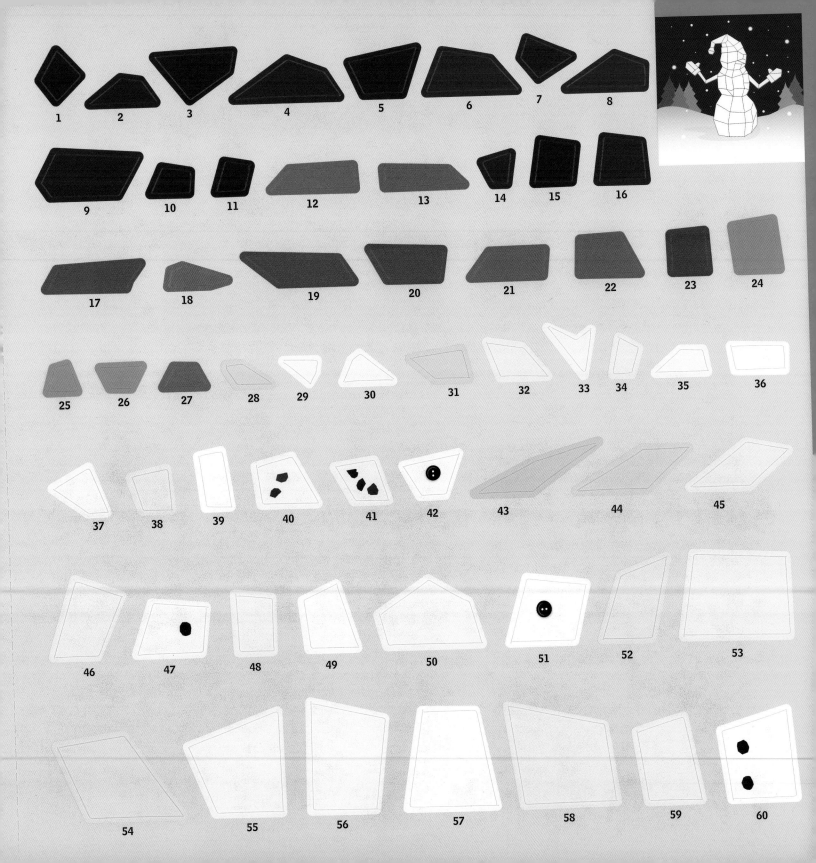